COOKING
with Fe

DELICIOUS FOOD MADE WITH LOVE

QUICK, EASY & FUN RECIPES ANYONE CAN COOK

FELISHA NICHOLSON

Cooking with Fe
Copyright 2024, Felisha Nicholson

PurposePals
hello@purposepalsllc.com

Printed in the United States of America.

ISBN: 979-8-9903589-4-2

TABLE OF CONTENTS

ABOUT CHEF FE

Chef Fe, a native of Tallahassee, Florida, is a self-taught home chef whose culinary journey began at an early age. With an unwavering passion for cooking, she views the kitchen as a sanctuary for creative expression and a platform for cultural exploration.

Driven by a profound love for global cuisine, Chef Fe embarked on a quest to immerse herself in diverse culinary traditions, constantly seeking to broaden her culinary horizons. In 2020, amidst the challenges of the COVID-19 pandemic, she seized the opportunity to share her culinary expertise by founding "The FE-Nomenal Experience, LLC." Specializing in in-home private dining experiences, Chef Fe and her team transformed dining into an unforgettable affair, complete with meticulously crafted meals, captivating tablescapes, and expertly documented memories through photography. Since its inception, "The FE-Nomenal Experience, LLC" has flourished into a multifaceted enterprise. Chef Fe's repertoire extends to event catering, virtual and in-person cooking classes, and engaging cooking camps tailored for aspiring young chefs.

Supported by a network of entrepreneurial family and friends, Chef Fe's dedication to her craft has garnered acclaim. In 2022 and 2023, "The FE-Nomenal Experience, LLC," was honored as "Caterer of the Year" in the Reader's Choice Awards for Tallahassee.

For Chef Fe, food transcends mere sustenance; it is a universal language that fosters connections and celebrates cultural diversity. With the belief that everyone shares a fundamental need to nourish both body and soul, Chef Fe's culinary mission embodies the notion that regardless of background or beliefs, food unites us all in the joy of shared experiences.

ACKNOWLEDGEMENTS

First and foremost, I would like to thank my Lord and Savior for ordering my steps and providing me with all that I have! Without God, there would be no me, and there would be no cookbook.

To my husband: Thank you for being my constant support, friend, lover, and accountability partner! Thank you for constantly pushing, loving, and motivating me to be my best self!

To my parents: Thank you for allowing me to be the creative person I am. During my years of life, you all have encouraged me to be and do what makes me happy! Growing up, I never felt boxed in and limited; I was able to be the free spirit that I am. Thank you to all four of you (Daddy, Mommy, Harold, and Denise)! Also, thanks to my "in-loves": Pops, Ma Rachel, and Mrs. Diane! Your encouragement and support will never go unnoticed!

To my siblings (Sylvia, Jonathan, and Javon): I genuinely have the best ones there ever could be! We stick together and love each other through it all! Thank you for having my back, listening, being a part of all my crazy (genius) ideas, and being so loving! And Drea, thank you for being an amazing SIL!

To my sweet bonus baby Makenzi: Watching you grow and having a passion for everything you do keeps me going! Your father and I hope to provide a life for you that continues giving, and we promise to encourage you to be the best person you can be!

OTHER ACKNOWLEDGMENTS AND SPECIAL RECOGNITION:

Publisher: PurposePals Publishing (Kimi Johnson)
Photographer: PhotosbyEnigmaSept
Recipe Content Development Assistance: Wendy Barber and Emanuel Nicholson
Cookbook Development Assistant: Qeahana Burrell
Staging and Wardrobe Styling: Sylvia Williams
Staging Assistants: Emanuel Nicholson, Muna Okoli, Nedra Randolph, and Denise Williams
Kitchen Set-Up/Location: Denise Williams
Makeup Artist: Kosmetic Diva (Keandra Clemons)
And to All my Family & Friends

Shrimp and Crab Avocado Toast   Serves 4

INGREDIENTS

½ pound of shrimp, chopped or small shrimp whole
½ cup lump crab meat
2 large avocados
2 plum tomatoes, diced
2 cups arugula
2 tbsp balsamic glaze
1 tbsp of Old Bay seasoning
1 tbsp olive oil
½ cup goat cheese

DIRECTIONS

1. Place a skillet on medium heat. Let it heat for a minute or two. Add 1 tbsp of olive oil. Sauté the shrimp with Old Bay seasoning until opaque. Add the crab meat. Sauté lightly for a minute. Remove from heat and set aside.

2. In a bowl, add the avocados without shell and pit. Smash the avocado. Add a sprinkle of salt and pepper, the diced tomatoes, and half of the lime juice. Gently mix the ingredients together.

3. Toast the sourdough bread in a toaster.

4. Once the sourdough bread is toasted, remove it from the toaster.

5. Lay the toasts flat on a plate. Spoon and spread the avocado mixture onto the toast in a flat layer.

6. Add some of the shrimp and crab mixture. Sprinkle some goat cheese and arugula on top of the slices. Then, drizzle some balsamic glaze on top for garnish (optional).

Fe's Tips and Tricks

Goat cheese provides a creamy element to the toast. However, you can use feta cheese instead or no cheese at all!

Balsamic Glaze gives this toast a slight acidic and a sweet element.

Any tomato will work for this recipe. I like plum tomatoes because they are firm and have a mild taste.

Creamy Stuffed Chicken

Serves 4

INGREDIENTS

4 chicken breasts
Olive oil
1 cup parmesan cheese (shaved or shredded)
8 oz cream cheese
1 tbsp garlic paste
1 tbsp sun-dried tomatoes
1 ½ cup spinach (cooked, drained, and cooled)
1 dash salt
1 dash pepper
1 tsp smoked paprika
1 tsp Morton Natures Seasoning Blend

ADDITIONAL TOOLS

Toothpicks

DIRECTIONS

1. Preheat oven to 375 degrees.

2. Butterfly chicken. Cut the chicken breasts horizontally, but leave the edges intact. Oil and season the chicken on the outside and inside. Use the seasoning blend and smoked paprika.

3. In a mixing bowl, add the cream cheese, spinach, parmesan cheese, sun-dried tomatoes, garlic paste, and a dash of salt & pepper. Mix until well blended.

4. Heat a large skillet on medium-high heat.

5. Using a small spoon or piping bag, add the filling inside of the butterflied chicken breasts. Use a few toothpicks to help seal the chicken breast shut.

6. Add 2 tbsps of olive oil to the skillet. Add the chicken breast to the skillet and sear on both sides of the breast until it has browned.

7. Place the chicken breast inside the heated oven and cook until the internal temperature of the breasts is 165 degrees and the filling is gooey.

8. Remove it from the oven and let it sit for a few minutes to help keep the juices circulating inside the chicken.

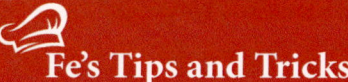

Fe's Tips and Tricks

Leftover cream cheese stuffing mixture? No problem! Add it to a small baking dish and bake it to make it into a dip!

Sage Butter Green Beans

INGREDIENTS

1 lb fresh green beans
Olive Oil
2 cups vegetable broth
2-3 tbsp salted butter
3 sage leaves
Salt & pepper to taste

DIRECTIONS

1. Place a large skillet on a large stove burner and turn the burner to medium heat. Let the skillet sit for 1-2 minutes. Add in olive oil.

2. Sauté the green beans in the skillet for a couple of minutes.

3. Add in vegetable broth, sage leaves, and butter. Gently sauté for 2 minutes.

4. Cover for an additional 6-8 minutes or until green beans are tender.

5. Salt and pepper to taste.

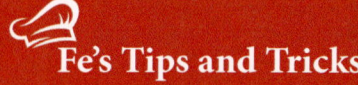

Fe's Tips and Tricks

Sage is a very aromatic herb. If you aren't used to cooking with sage, try using 1-2 leaves and then add an additional one if you'd like.

Rosemary and thyme are also delightful herbs with green beans.

Creamy Garlic Mashed Potatoes

Serves 4-6

INGREDIENTS

10 red potatoes
8 garlic cloves
2 bay leaves
6 cups vegetable broth
½ stick salted butter
½ cup heavy whipping cream
Salt
Black pepper

DIRECTIONS

1. Empty one container of vegetable broth in a large pot. If the vegetable broth doesn't fill the pot halfway, use water to fill the remainder. Boil the liquid.

2. Chop 10 red potatoes into small chunks. Add the chopped potatoes, garlic, and bay leaves to the pot of water. Gently stir and then boil until tender.

3. Stir occasionally so the potatoes do not stick to the bottom of the pot.

4. When potatoes are tender, set aside a cup of the starchy potato water. The remaining water can be drained.

5. Smash the potatoes. Add heavy whipping cream, ¼ cup of starchy water, and butter. Mix until butter melts.

6. Stir and add the liquid measurements until the potatoes reach the desired consistency.

7. Salt and pepper to taste.

Fe's Tips and Tricks

Using a potato masher isn't required to make mashed potatoes. However, it sure makes it a lot easier to smash the potatoes. Of course, you could use a large spoon or even a fork.

You could also use chicken broth instead of vegetable broth when boiling the potatoes for more flavor. Cooking potatoes with the broth really builds in a lot of flavor.

Peaches and Cream French Toast   Serves 6

INGREDIENTS

Sliced brioche loaf
6 Eggs
1 ½ cups heavy whipping cream
1 tsp vanilla extract
1 cup brown sugar
3 tsp ground cinnamon
4 small cans of peaches with syrup
½ stick salted butter
½ tsp salt
1 can of whipped cream topping
Canola oil spray
Mint (optional)

DIRECTIONS

1. In a saucepan, add a stick of butter. Allow it to melt completely on medium heat. Add cans of peaches, 1 tsp cinnamon, brown sugar, salt, and vanilla extract.

2. Prepare your French toast batter by combining 4 eggs and heavy whipping cream. Gently whisk those ingredients together in a bowl. Add 2 tsp of cinnamon and a pinch of salt. Mix together.

3. Heat skillet or griddle on medium heat. Once heated, spray skillet or griddle with canola oil spray or add butter.

4. Gently dip the sliced brioche bread (one at a time) into the batter on both sides. Then, gently lay the bread onto the skillet or griddle in a single layer. Allow the French toast to cook on each side for about a minute or two until golden brown. Do this until all slices of French toast have been prepared.

5. Assemble the French toast by cutting it into halves and placing two halves (two slices of toast) on a plate. Top the French toast with the peach mixture. If you'd like, add a dollop of whipped cream and a sprig of mint for additional garnish.

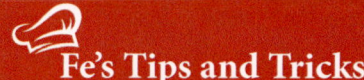

Fe's Tips and Tricks

I love to use heavy whipping cream to make my batter for French toast. However, you could use milk instead. If you're vegan, you could use a milk and egg substitute.

This French toast is very decadent. One to two slices per person is probably sufficient!

Easy Sausage Casserole

Serves 6-8

INGREDIENTS

16 oz ground sausage
6 eggs
2 cups milk
2 tbsp olive oil
1 ½ tsp salt
1 tsp dried chives
1 tsp pepper
½ bag of frozen shredded hashbrowns
2 cups of your choice of cheese

DIRECTIONS

1. Preheat the oven to 350 degrees.

2. Heat a skillet on medium heat. Add in olive oil.

3. Add in one roll of ground sausage. Crumble and cook sausage until it's done (no more pink/red coloring). Then, set aside off of the hot burner.

4. In a large bowl, whisk eggs and milk together. Add in salt, chives, and pepper. Mix.

5. Inside the casserole dish, add half the bag of shredded hashbrowns (about 13 oz). Then mix in the sausage and cheese of your choice. Make sure it's well blended.

6. Add in the egg mixture, make sure it's well mixed. Sprinkle with ½ tsp of salt.

7. Put in the oven for about 40-45 minutes until the dish is bubbly and not jiggly in the center. You could also test it by sticking a fork or skewer inside the center. If it comes off clean with no liquid egg mixture, it's done.

Fe's Tips and Tricks

Sausage casseroles are super easy to make! You could use any protein you'd like and even throw in some diced veggies! Try different variations!

You could also pour the casserole mixture into muffin sections in a muffin pan, make individual servings, and freeze them for later! Once cooked, they'll also be good in the fridge for about 3 days.

Pasta Pomodoro

Serves 6

INGREDIENTS

1 can of crushed tomatoes
4 fresh basil leaves
2 tbsp garlic
1 cup yellow onion
1 lb spaghetti noodles
1 tsp salt
1 tsp olive oil
1 tsp red pepper flakes
1 tsp sugar
Parmesan cheese

Fe's Tips and Tricks

Adding a dash of sugar to red sauces helps to reduce the acidity in the sauce you taste.

One way to check if your spaghetti noodles are done is to cut one in half. The noodle is done if the spaghetti is opaque in the center and has no white ring or spot.

DIRECTIONS

1. Place a large pot or deep skillet onto the large burner of the stove.

2. Turn the burner on to medium heat. Let sit for a few minutes, then add in olive oil.

3. Add in chopped yellow onions. Sauté until the onions are tender.

4. Pour in a can of crushed tomatoes. Stir. Add in salt and sugar. Stir.

5. Add in basil leaves, red pepper flakes, and garlic. Stir.

6. Taste and add more salt, sugar, or pepper as needed. Let simmer on med-low for about 10 minutes. Stir occasionally.

For the pasta:

1. Fill a large pot about halfway with water, and place on a large burner on the stove.

2. Add a tbsp of salt to the water. Boil the water on high heat. When water is boiling, gently add in the noodles. Stir.

3. Once the noodles are al dente, set aside ½ cup of pasta water, remove the pasta from the heat, and drain.

4. Add the noodles and ¼ cup of pasta water to the sauce and stir. Sprinkle with some parmesan cheese and additional basil for garnish.

Moroccan Shakshuka

Serves 6

INGREDIENTS

1 tbsp harissa
1 tbsp ras el hanout
1 tbsp saffron
6 eggs
1 tbsp tomato paste
1 tsp turmeric
½ cup red bell pepper, chopped
½ cup yellow bell pepper, chopped
½ cup orange bell peppers, chopped
½ cup yellow onion, chopped
2 tbsp of minced garlic
14.5 oz can of diced tomatoes
28 oz can of crushed tomatoes
1 tbsp cumin
1 tsp salt
1 tbsp olive oil
Cilantro

DIRECTIONS

1. Heat a large skillet or dutch oven over medium heat.

2. Add two tablespoons of olive oil. Then, add red bell peppers, yellow bell peppers, orange bell peppers, and yellow onion. Sauté for about a minute.

3. Add in a tomato paste, salt, and harissa paste. Stir until well blended. Continue to cook the vegetables until the onion becomes translucent.

4. Add a can of diced tomatoes, turmeric, and a can of crushed tomatoes (including the liquid). Stir. Let the sauce simmer uncovered for about 8-10 minutes while the sauce thickens. Salt to taste.

5. Use a ladle, spoon, or spatula to create a little nest in the sauce for the eggs. Gently crack the eggs into the nests. Once you have all the eggs, you can cover them to allow the eggs to cook. Cook as long as you want until the eggs are your desired preference. However, the best shakshuka has runny eggs.

6. Sprinkle the shakshuka with a little parsley and cilantro for garnish. You can even add some creamy feta or goat cheese on top.

7. This dish is best served with some bread for dipping (pita, labneh, or naan).

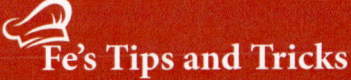

Fe's Tips and Tricks

Harissa, ras el hanout, and saffron can be found in specialty stores and markets or can be ordered from Amazon.

Harissa paste and saffron powder will work best for this recipe.

Chermoula Shrimp & Veggie Skewers

Serves 6

INGREDIENTS

1 tsp Harissa	1 tsp ground
1 lb shrimp	ginger
1 lb zucchini, wedged	1 tsp turmeric
1 lb squash, wedged	1 tsp salt
1 tsp smoked paprika	¼ cup lemon juice
Water	¼ cup olive oil
½ yellow onion,	Black pepper
chunked	3 cups cilantro
6-8 garlic cloves	1 cup parsley
1 tsp ground cumin	

ADDITIONAL TOOLS

Skewers
Basting brush

DIRECTIONS

Chermoula Marinade

1. In a food processor, add cilantro and parsley. Then add lemon, olive oil, salt, turmeric, ginger, harissa, garlic, and smoked paprika. (Add water if needed.)

2. Give a few puree pulses until it reaches the correct consistency (pestoey). Refrigerate marinade until needed.

Chermoula Shrimp & Vegetable Skewers

1. Add shrimp and veggies to skewers. Using a basting brush, slather the shrimp and veggies with the chermoula marinade. Sprinkle with salt and pepper.

2. Roast the zucchini, squash, and onions in the oven at 475 degrees for about 12-14 minutes or until tender (flipping halfway). Once you flip the vegetables, add the shrimp to the oven to cook the remainder of the time with them. Once the shrimp and veggies are cooked, remove them from the oven.

Fe's Tips and Tricks

The chermoula marinade can be used for just about any protein! You can use it to marinate fish, shrimp, lamb, pork chops, chicken, etc. It can also be used as a chimichurri sauce for steak!

Serve this dish with rice, lemon wedge, and extra chermoula, if desired.

Lobster Bisque

Serves 4

INGREDIENTS

1 can cream corn
6 tbsp salted butter
½ cup green onion
½ cup flour
Vegetable broth
1 pint heavy cream
1-2 tbsp Old Bay
1 tsp black pepper
1 tbsp roasted garlic paste
1 tbsp sea salt
1-2 tbsp paprika
1 tsp red pepper flakes
1 tbsp celery seeds
1 lb Langostino lobster

DIRECTIONS

1. Heat a large pot on medium heat. Add in salted butter. Once the salted butter melts, add in green onion. Saute for about a minute, and then add flour. Stir until it becomes pasty. Add in creamed corn. Pour in heavy cream. Stir until the liquid is smooth and begins to thicken.

2. Add Old Bay seasoning, celery seeds, sea salt, black pepper, and red chili flakes. Stir until the seasoning is well blended with the bisque mixture. Add paprika until the bisque is a pale pink color. Taste and add additional seasoning to your liking.

3. Add lobster meat. If your bisque is too thick, add a little vegetable broth until it reaches your preferred consistency. Garnish with puff pastry and/or chives. Enjoy.

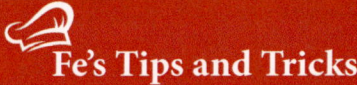

Fe's Tips and Tricks

This lobster bisque is very creamy and rich! You could sub the lobster for crab, and it now becomes a crab bisque! If using crab, go for the lump crab. You'll thank me later!

Be sure to taste periodically to check for the desired salt amount. Several ingredients contain salt, so you may not need to add much. Sprinkle and taste as you go.

Pineapple Salmon Boats
Serves 1-2

INGREDIENTS

2 whole pineapples
2 tbsp minced garlic
1 green bell pepper, chopped
1 red bell pepper, chopped
1 orange bell pepper, chopped
1 yellow bell pepper, chopped
Olive oil
1 whole red onion, chopped
1 tbsp Sazon seasoning
1 can pigeon peas
3 cups pre-cooked rice, cooled
1 tsp black pepper
Creole seasoning
1 tbsp turmeric

6 ¼ cup sweetened coconut, shredded
1 cup pineapple, diced (this will come from the 2 whole pineapples)
1 tbsp jalapeno, chopped and deseeded
¼ cup cilantro
1 tsp sea salt
1 lime, juiced
¼ cup fresh squeezed orange juice
4 salmon filets

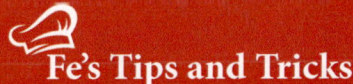

Fe's Tips and Tricks

You can use the frozen pineapples for my Tropi-Co-Lada Smoothie on page 101.

DIRECTIONS

1. Cut the pineapple in half lengthwise, leaving the leaves on. Remove the core. Cut the pineapple into cubes with a knife and scoop them out with a spoon. Now you have a pineapple boat!

2. Dice the pineapple chunks. Set 1½ cup of the pineapples to the side, and freeze the rest! (See Chef Fe's Tips and Tricks)

3. Add garlic and 1 tbsp of olive oil in a heated large pot or wok. Add ½ of the red, yellow, orange, and green bell pepper. Then, add ½ the red onion and ½ cup of pigeon peas, and sauté for a couple of minutes.

4. Then, add the pre-cooked rice. Stir until the rice, peppers, peas, and onion are well-blended and well-heated. Turn down the heat to a lower heat setting. Add the Sazon, creole seasoning, black pepper, and turmeric. Stir. Then, add a half cup of diced pineapple and the shredded coconut. Stir until blended in. Remove from heat.

5. In a medium bowl, add a cup of diced pineapple, the jalapeño, and the other halves of all four colors of the bell peppers and red onion. Stir.

6. Then, add a tbsp of olive oil, cilantro, black pepper, and sea salt. Stir. Add in lime juice and ¼ fresh squeezed orange juice. Stir and refrigerate until ready to serve.

7. Preheat oven to 375 degrees. Lay parchment paper on a baking sheet or grease the baking sheet with olive oil. Drizzle the bottom of the salmon with a little olive oil and sprinkle with some Creole seasoning. Lay it on the baking sheet. Flip the salmon over and sprinkle the top of the salmon pieces with Creole seasoning. Bake for 15-20 minutes (USDA recommended internal temp 145 degrees.)

8. To assemble, add the rice to the pineapple boats. Then, add a filet of salmon. Lastly, add 1 tbsp of pineapple salsa on top of the salmon filet.

Crispy Sticky Wings

Serves 6-8

INGREDIENTS

2 tbsp hoisin
2 tbsp green onion, chopped
½ tsp sesame oil
1 tbsp fresh squeezed lime juice
3 tbsp soy sauce
½ tbsp oyster sauce
⅓ cup ketchup
3 tbsp dark brown sugar
1 tbsp sweet chili sauce
1 tbsp ginger
1 tbsp sliced fresh chili
1 tbsp garlic paste
½ tsp Chinese 5 Spice
1 tbsp sesame seeds
3 lb chicken wing sections

DIRECTIONS

1. Preheat the fryer to 350 degrees.

2. In a medium bowl, mix the sesame oil, lemon juice, soy sauce, garlic paste, brown sugar, hoisin, oyster sauce, ketchup, sweet chili sauce, five spice and ginger.

3. Add the sauce to a medium saucepan and heat on medium heat. Stir until the sauce thickens and the brown sugar dissolves.

4. Fry chicken wings until the wings reach an internal temperature of 165 degrees. Set aside.

5. Gently coat the wings with the sauce. Garnish the wings with sesame seeds, green onion, and sliced chili pepper.

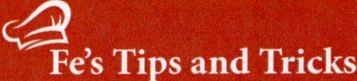

Fe's Tips and Tricks

If you want an even crispier coat of wings, sprinkle them with some cornstarch before frying.

You could also prepare the wings in an air fryer or fry them over the stove instead of in the deep fryer. If you're frying them over the stove, check the oil temperature to ensure it is 350 degrees.

Ginger Miso Soup

Serves 2-4

INGREDIENTS

¼ cup Miso paste
1 tsp ginger, chopped or ginger paste
4 cups vegetable broth
1 cup firm tofu, diced
1 cup dried nori/seaweed
2 scallion green onion, thinly sliced
Soy sauce

DIRECTIONS

1. In a medium saucepan, bring vegetable broth to a boil.

2. Reduce heat to low, and add the miso paste, 1 tsp of soy sauce, and ginger. Stir until well mixed and the miso paste is dissolved.

3. Add half of the green onion and the tofu. Stir.

4. Add small pieces of nori/seaweed. Stir.

5. Taste. Add in additional miso and soy sauce, as desired.

6. Serve with an additional garnish of green onions on top.

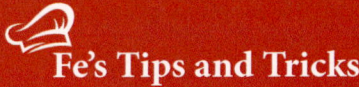

Fe's Tips and Tricks

Ginger is great for gut health and adds a pleasant spice to the miso soup.

Tagliatelle al Ragu

Serves 6-8

INGREDIENTS

2 celery stalks, diced
½ cup carrots, shredded
Sea salt
2 tbsp olive oil
1 tsp sugar
1 lb ground Italian sausage
1 lb ground beef
4 oz garlic paste
10 basil leaves
¾ cup red wine
1 cup cremini mushrooms, chopped
2 tbsp chopped parsley
2 cans of 28 oz crushed tomatoes
1 lb tagliatelle
1 large yellow onion, chopped

DIRECTIONS

1. Heat a large pot over medium heat. Let it heat for a couple of minutes. Add olive oil. Then, add celery and onion.

2. Sautè until the onions and celery are slightly tender. Add the ground beef and sausage. Cook until browned. Add additional oil if needed.

3. Add in the shredded carrot. Sautè for a couple more minutes. Add in the red wine. Stir.

4. Add in both cans of crushed tomatoes. Stir. Then, add the garlic paste, basil leaves, and a tsp of salt. Stir. Cover and let simmer on low heat for about 10-15 minutes.

5. Add in sugar and the cremini mushrooms. Stir and let simmer for about 5 minutes.

6. In a separate large pot, boil tagliatelle pasta in salted water until tender. Once pasta is tender, reserve ½ cup of pasta water. Drain the remaining pasta from the water.

7. Add the reserved pasta water to the sauce. Stir and taste. Add additional salt, if needed.

8. Gently add the cooked tagliatelle to the ragu sauce and fold in until well-blended.

9. Serve with a parsley garnish, and enjoy!

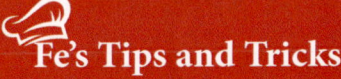

Fe's Tips and Tricks

Don't eat red meat? Sub for grounded turkey and/or turkey sausage.

If it's too large of a portion, no problem! You can make and freeze this dish.

Calamares Fritos

INGREDIENTS

1 lb thawed calamari rings
1 whole lemon, wedged
1 tsp salt
1 tsp black pepper
2 tbsp onion powder
2 tbsp garlic powder
½ tsp of cayenne pepper
¼ cup of hot sauce
Canola oil
⅓ cup corn starch
1 tsp baking powder
2 cups all-purpose flour
2 cups buttermilk

Fe's Tips and Tricks

The buttermilk marinade adheres to the flour and tenderizes the calamari. The longer the calamari marinates, the more tender they become. Skipping this step could cause your calamari to be tough.

Just like fried shrimp, calamari doesn't take long to cook. A couple of minutes in the oil is enough.

DIRECTIONS

1. In a large bowl, add the calamari rings, buttermilk, and hot sauce. Gently stir. Cover tightly with saran wrap and store in the fridge for about 30 minutes to an hour.

2. In a separate bowl, add the flour, baking powder, and cornstarch. Gently mix. Add in garlic powder, onion powder, pepper and salt.

3. Fill your fryer or a large deep cast iron skillet with canola oil, enough to deep fry. Using a kitchen thermometer, heat oil until it reaches 350 degrees.

4. Remove calamari rings from the refrigerator.

5. Gently add a few rings at a time to the flour mixture. Toss until well coated. (The buttermilk marinade acts as the flour's adhesion mechanism). Set aside the flour-coated calamari on a baking sheet with a baking rack. Keep going until all the calamari are battered.

6. Gently lower a few rings of calamari into the oil and fry until crispy. Flip on both sides to ensure even cooking. Set the fried calamari rings aside on another baking rack or a plate with paper towels to drain excess oil.

7. Serve with lemon wedges.

Honey Sriracha Salmon

Serves 4

INGREDIENTS

4 filets of wild-caught Pacific salmon (skin-on)
Garlic powder
Salt
Black pepper
¼ cup honey
¼ cup sriracha
Olive oil

DIRECTIONS

1. Preheat the oven to 400 degrees.

2. In a small bowl, add sriracha and honey. Place fillets on a baking sheet. Drizzle both sides of the fillets with olive oil.

3. Sprinkle the meat side of the filets with salt, pepper, and garlic powder.

4. Using a basting brush, slather the meat side of the filets with the honey sriracha sauce.

5. Bake in the oven for 10-15 minutes or until the salmon is cooked with an instant-read of 135 degrees internal temperature on the kitchen thermometer.

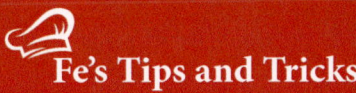

Fe's Tips and Tricks

Wild-caught Pacific Salmon is known to be the healthiest salmon to consume.

I love to serve this salmon with my Creamy Garlic Mashed Potatoes (page 17) and Sage Butter Green Beans (page 15).

Crispy Black Bean Cakes

Serves 4

INGREDIENTS

1 can black refried beans
1 can black beans, drained
1 tbsp garlic paste
1 cup bread crumbs
1 egg
½ cup flour
1 tbsp creole seasoning
¼ cup cilantro, chopped
2 plum tomatoes, diced
¼ red onion, chopped
1 tsp jalapeño, diced
1 tsp garlic, minced
1 small container of sour cream
1 tsp salt
1 tsp pepper
¼ cup canola oil
1 tsp cumin
1 tsp onion powder
1 lime

Fe's Tips and Tricks

Vegan? No problem! Nix the eggs and use an egg replacement or vegan mayo. You could also nix the sour cream and just have the pico!

Greek yogurt could also be used instead of sour cream.

DIRECTIONS

Pico de Gallo

1. Add the tomatoes, red onion, lime juice, 2 tbsp cilantro, jalapeno, and a sprinkle of salt and pepper in a medium bowl. Mix. Set aside in the refrigerator.

Black Bean Cakes

1. In another large bowl, add the refried beans. Loosen the beans with a spoon by stirring with 1 tsp of water. Add the drained black beans, garlic paste, egg, creole seasoning, cumin, and onion powder, and sprinkle in salt and pepper. Mix with a spoon.

2. In the bowl with the black bean mixture, add the bread crumbs. Gently fold the crumbs into the black bean mixture. The black bean mixture should be wet, but thick enough to form into patties.

3. Grease a baking sheet or lay a sheet of parchment paper on it. Using a large ice cream scoop, scoop some of the black bean mixture into your hands. Form it into a ball, then gently press down until it forms a patty. Lay the patty on the baking sheet. Repeat these steps until all the patties are formed.

4. Refrigerate for 30 minutes to an hour until the patties are firm.

5. Preheat the oven to 375 degrees. Heat a large skillet on the stove with ¼ cup of canola oil. Sprinkle both sides of the patties with flour. Lay the patties inside the skillet in a single layer. (Do not overcrowd the skillet). Sear on both sides until browned and crispy. Once all the patties have been browned on both sides, place them in the oven to continue to cook for 10-15 minutes.

6. Serve patties with the refrigerated homemade pico and a dollop of sour cream.

Chopped Cheese Sliders

INGREDIENTS

12 sweet Hawaiian slider rolls
1 tbsp garlic paste
1 tbsp dried parsley flakes
1 stick salted butter
1 lb ground beef
½ cup shredded cheddar, mild
12 slices American cheese
1 cup ketchup
¼ cup yellow mustard
½ tbsp seasoning salt
2 tsp cumin
1 tbsp onion powder
2 tbsp sweet relish
Olive oil
¼ cup green bell pepper, diced
¼ cup yellow onion, diced

DIRECTIONS

1. Heat a large skillet over medium heat for a couple of minutes. Add 2 tbsp of olive oil. Then, add in the ground beef. Use a spoon or spatula to separate the ground beef in the skillet.

2. Add the green bell pepper, yellow onion, seasoning salt, garlic powder, onion powder, black pepper, and cumin. Continue to cook ground beef for a few minutes until it is completely browned.

3. Add ketchup, yellow mustard, relish, and shredded cheese. Stir in with the beef until the cheese is melted.

4. Split the Hawaiian buns in half. Lay the bottom halves side by side onto a baking sheet.

5. Add the ground beef mixture to the bottom of the Hawaiian buns, then place sliced American cheese on top. Place the top half of the buns on top of the cheese.

6. In a small bowl, melt one stick of butter in the microwave for 45 seconds. Add in garlic paste and parsley. Mix.

7. Butter the top of the sliders with a basting brush. Bake at 350 degrees until the cheese is melted.

Fe's Tips and Tricks

You can use any ground meat for these sliders (ground chicken, pork, veggie, turkey, etc.)

If you are vegetarian, use a meat substitute like ground vegetable crumbles.

Gambas al Ajillo
Shrimp with Garlic Sauce

Serves 2-4

INGREDIENTS

10 cloves of garlic
1 pound of shrimp
1 small piece of dried guajillo chile
1 tsp of sherry vinegar
¼ tsp baking soda
Extra virgin olive oil
¼ cup fresh parsley, chopped
½ lemon
Salt
Garlic toast points (optional)

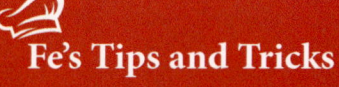

Fe's Tips and Tricks

Step 3 is essential to this dish because it helps the shrimp to become juicy and tender.

The fresher and larger the shrimp, the better! You can use jumbo or colossal shrimp instead of large shrimp.

Choose red chili pepper flakes if you can't find a guajillo chile.

DIRECTIONS

1. Mince half of the garlic cloves and slice the other half. Peel shrimp. Place peeled shrimp in a bowl. Leave shells aside in a separate bowl. (Do not disgard shrimp shells).

2. Add the minced garlic, a sprinkle of salt, baking soda, and 3 tbsp of olive oil in the bowl with the shrimp. Gently toss until the ingredients are mixed together. Set aside.

3. Heat a large skillet on medium heat for about 2 minutes. Add 4 tbsp of olive oil. Then, add the shrimp shells, guajillo chile, and a tbsp of the sliced garlic cloves. Saute until the shells are red and the oil is aromatic.

4. Using a fine mesh strainer, separate the aromatic oil from the shells, garlic, and pepper. Discard the pepper, shells, and garlic.

5. Return the aromatic oil to the skillet and heat over medium heat. Add remaining sliced garlic and shrimp. Saute the shrimp until opaque (about 2 minutes). Add the juice of half of the lemon, sherry vinegar, and parsley. Toss gently. Season to taste with salt. Serve with some garlic toast points.

Butter Pecan French Toast

Serves 6

INGREDIENTS

Sliced brioche loaf
6 eggs
2 cups heavy cream
2 tbsp cinnamon
¼ cup chopped pecans
Canola spray
Sea salt
1 stick salted butter
1 cup dark brown sugar
1 can of whipped cream topping
Powdered sugar

Fe's Tips and Tricks

I love to use heavy whipping cream to make my batter for French toast. However, you could use milk instead. If you're vegan, you could use a milk and egg substitute.

This French toast is very decadent. One to two slices per person is probably sufficient!

DIRECTIONS

1. In a saucepan, add a stick of butter. Allow it to melt completely on medium heat. Add in brown sugar. Mix until the brown sugar and butter are blended. Add heavy cream and a pinch of salt. Stir until the brown sugar has dissolved. Add in more cream to assist the sauce in getting to the desired consistency. Add in pecans. Let sit for one minute on very low heat.

2. Prepare the French toast batter by combining eggs and 1½ cups of heavy whipping cream in a bowl. Gently whisk those ingredients together. Add cinnamon. Mix together.

3. Heat skillet or a griddle on medium heat.

4. Once heated, spray the skillet or griddle with canola oil or add butter. Gently dip the sliced brioche bread (one at a time) into the batter on both sides. Then, gently lay the bread into the skillet or onto the griddle in a single layer. Allow the French toast to cook on each side for 1-2 minutes, until golden brown. Repeat until all slices of French toast have been prepared.

5. Assemble the French toast by cutting the toast into halves, placing 4 halves (two slices of toast) on a plate. Top the French toast with the butter pecan sauce. Feel free to add more pecans if you'd like. Sprinkle with powdered sugar, add a dollop of whipped cream on top and a sprig of mint for an additional garnish.

Easy Seafood Strata

Serves 6

INGREDIENTS

½ pound crawfish
½ small shrimp
1 pound lump crab meat
1 loaf challah bread, cubed
2 cups heavy whipping cream or milk
1 tsp ground mustard
½ cup medium yellow onion, diced
½ cup medium red pepper, chopped
6 large eggs
¼ green onions, chopped
1 tbsp Old Bay seasoning
1 tsp black pepper
1 tsp sea salt
3 tbsp salted butter
1 tsp chili pepper flakes
1 cup smoked gouda cheese, shredded
1 cup cheddar cheese, shredded

DIRECTIONS

1. Heat a skillet on medium heat. Add in salted butter. Add in a pound of small shrimp. Sauté for just a couple of minutes. Add crawfish, lump crab meat, and Old Bay seasoning with the shrimp. Sauté.

2. In a bowl, crack and gently whisk 6 eggs. Add heavy whipping cream or milk, sea salt, Old Bay, chili flakes, ground mustard, and pepper. Whisk together. Set aside. (This can be done the night before.)

3. Preheat oven to 375 degrees.

4. Add 1 loaf of cubed challah bread, red bell pepper, yellow onion, green onion, shredded gouda cheese, and shredded cheddar cheese in a large separate bowl. Gently toss them together. Then, combine the seafood mixture with the bread mixture.

5. Add the bread mixture to a greased large casserole dish (13x9 dish would work). Evenly distribute the egg mixture on top of the bread mixture. Sprinkle a little more smoked gouda and/or cheddar cheese.

6. Bake in the oven for 40 minutes or until the Strata is cooked. The center shouldn't be jiggly. Use a knife to check if it is cooked in the center. Gently insert the knife into the center of the dish, and if it comes out clean, it's good to go.

7. Take the strata out and allow it to sit for a few minutes before serving.

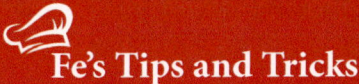

Fe's Tips and Tricks

You can use whatever seafood you'd like for this recipe. Make it your own!

Scallop Ceviche

INGREDIENTS

1 lb bay scallops (small) or cut the large scallops into smaller chunks
½ cup fresh squeezed lime juice
¼ cup fresh orange juice
Salt
Black pepper
1 hothouse cucumber, seeded, diced
½ cup scallions/green onion, chopped
¼ cup fresh parsley, chopped
1 ½ tbsp jalapeno, seeded
2 tbsp fresh garlic, chopped
½ cup red bell pepper, chopped
¼ cup yellow bell pepper, chopped
¼ cup orange bell pepper, chopped
¼ cup olive oil

Garnish Options
Butter lettuce
Plantain chips
Crackers
Avocado

DIRECTIONS

1. Add all ingredients to a large mixing bowl. Gently toss the ingredients. Salt and pepper to taste.

2. Refrigerate for one to two hours before serving.

3. Serve with garnish option of choice.

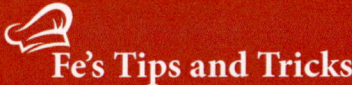

Fe's Tips and Tricks

If you can not find small bay scallops, you can cut large scallops into smaller chunks.

This ceviche is best served fresh! However, you can store it in your fridge for up to two days after preparation.

Crab Stuffed Shrimp

INGREDIENTS

8 oz container of claw or lump crab meat
1 sleeve of crushed Ritz crackers
1 pound of extra large shrimp thawed and deveined (15-20 count)
2 tbsp Dijon mustard
¼ cup mayo
2 tbsp fresh squeezed lemon juice
1 tbsp Old Bay Seasoning
2 tbsp fresh or dried chives
½ melted butter
1 tbsp creole seasoning
Black pepper
Olive oil

DIRECTIONS

1. Preheat oven to 425 degrees. Add the crab meat, crushed crackers, Old Bay seasoning, black pepper (to taste), and chives in a large mixing bowl. Gently mix the ingredients together.

2. In a separate bowl, add Dijon mustard, mayo, and lemon juice. Mix, then add to crab mixture and gently toss.

3. Drizzle the shrimp with olive oil.

4. Spray or spread olive oil onto a baking sheet. Butterfly/split the bottom of the shrimp so that it sits on top of the baking sheet. Do this for all shrimp.

5. Add a spoonful of the crab mixture on each shrimp and fold the tail over so that it lays on top of the stuffing.

6. Sprinkle the creole seasoning on top of the shrimp.

7. Bake the shrimp for 15 minutes. When the shrimp is cooked.

8. When the shrimp is cooked, remove them from the oven and brush with melted butter.

Fe's Tips and Tricks

I recommend serving these Crab-stuffed Shrimp with some of my Creamy Garlic Mashed Potatoes (page 17) and Sage Butter Green Beans (page 15)!

Creamy Seafood Linguine

Serves 8

INGREDIENTS

1 lb tail-on shrimp, peeled and deveined
1 lb lump crab meat
½ lb rinsed crawfish meat
1 cup red onion, diced
2 tbsp garlic paste
2 tbsp basil pesto
1 lb linguine
1 cup parmesan, shaved
2 cups heavy cream
4 fresh basil leaves, shredded
2 tbsp salted butter or olive oil
½ tsp red pepper flakes
Salt
Black pepper

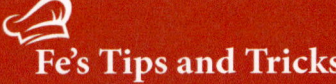

Fe's Tips and Tricks

Leaving the tails on shrimp will aid the shrimp in maintaining their size and locking in flavor and moisture.

Crawfish can have a strong aroma. Rinsing the meat before adding it to the dish can reduce its pungency.

DIRECTIONS

1. In a large pot, add water to boil your noodles. Salt the water. Once boiling, add the noodles. Stir. Once the noodles are tender (al dente), remove them from the stove and drain.

2. Heat a skillet or saucepan on medium heat. Add 1 tbsp of butter or olive oil. Once the butter has melted, add red onion. Add pesto and sprinkle in the red pepper flakes. Then, add heavy cream and garlic paste. Stir until the cream begins to thicken. Turn down the heat to medium-low.

3. Add in shaved parmesan. Mix until well blended. Taste and add salt and black pepper, as desired. Then, add in the lump crab and crawfish meat. Mix and turn the sauce to low heat.

4. While the sauce is simmering on low, heat a separate skillet on medium heat. Add 1 tbsp of melted butter or olive oil. Season shrimp with ½ salt and ½ black pepper. Sauté shrimp on both sides until pink. Once cooked, set the shrimp aside.

5. Add linguine and shrimp into the sauce and gently toss until evenly coated. Garnish with shaved parmesan and basil if you'd like.

Crustless Breakfast Quiche

Serves 4

INGREDIENTS

12 eggs
½ cup heavy cream
1 lb linked smoked sausage
¼ cup red pepper, chopped
¼ cup green pepper, chopped
¼ cup red onion, chopped
10 oz spinach
1 tsp salt
1 tsp black pepper
Garlic cloves, minced
Canola oil spray

Fe's Tips and Tricks

You can freeze the crustless quiches to make breakfast ahead. Thaw and warm when ready to serve.

If using ground breakfast meat, brown and cool the meat before adding it to the egg mixture.

Serve with a side of my Smoked Gouda Grits (page 63).

This recipe can also be enjoyed meatless.

DIRECTIONS

1. Spray a muffin pan with canola oil spray.

2. Preheat oven to 375 degrees.

3. Begin making the egg mixture by cracking a dozen eggs into a mixing bowl. Add in heavy cream, then whisk together.

4. Shred the spinach and add it to the egg mixture.

5. Add red pepper, green pepper, red onion, and garlic to the egg mixture.

6. Chop the sausage (or meat of your choice) and add it to the egg mixture.

7. Lightly mix ingredients until everything is well incorporated.

8. Using a ladle, fill each muffin pan cup up about ¾ of the way with the egg mixture.

9. Bake in the oven for 30-35 minutes or until the egg mixture is cooked through and set.

Buffalo Chicken Deviled Eggs

8-12 Servings

INGREDIENTS

12 large boiled and peeled eggs
¼ cup mayo
¼ cup ranch
2 tbsp dried chives
2 tbsp blue cheese crumbles
½ cup rotisserie chicken, chopped
1 tsp garlic powder
3 tbsp buffalo sauce
Salt
Black pepper

DIRECTIONS

1. Halve the boiled eggs. Carefully scoop out the yolk into a separate bowl. Leave the whites to the side on a separate platter.

2. Using a fork, mash the yolks until they are a crumb consistency. Add the mayo, ranch, and buffalo sauce. Gently mix until the yolks are smooth and creamy.

3. Gently fold in the dried chives and chicken. Add the garlic powder and a sprinkle of salt and black pepper.

4. Insert the deviled egg mixture into a piping bag or gallon-sized Ziploc bag. (If using a Ziploc bag, cut a corner of the bag and pipe the mixture into the eggs.)

5. Sprinkle with blue cheese crumbles for garnish.

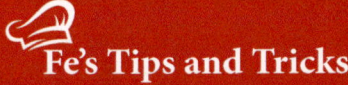

Fe's Tips and Tricks

There are so many tricks to peeling eggs! My favorite way is to add the shelled eggs in a container with a little water and gently shake them. The shells fall right off!

If you don't want to worry about peeling eggs, you can buy them already boiled from the store! You can also purchase a rotisserie chicken from the store and use that as the chicken for the deviled eggs.

If you want the Buffalo Chicken Deviled Eggs to have a looser consistency, add more ranch to the egg mixture.

Smoked Gouda Grits

Serves 4

INGREDIENTS

1 ½ cup grits
1 cup shredded Smoked Gouda cheese
1 tbsp salt
1 tsp black pepper
Heavy cream
1 tbsp salted butter
6 ¼ cup water

DIRECTIONS

1. In a pot, add water, butter, and salt. Boil.

2. When the water boils, slowly whisk in the grits. Whisking in the grits too quickly will result in lumpy, uncooked grits. Turn the heat down to low. Cover the grits and stir often.

3. Once the grits begin to thicken and the water is mostly absorbed, add half of the Smoked Gouda cheese and slowly whisk in heavy cream until the grits are creamy.

4. Add salt and black pepper to taste.

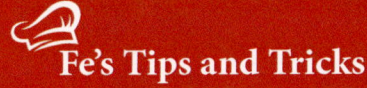

Fe's Tips and Tricks

Grits are unforgiving when there is too much salt. Be sure to add a little, then taste a little.

Italian Red Sauce

Serves 4

INGREDIENTS

1 can crushed tomatoes
4 fresh basil leaves
2 tbsp garlic paste
1 cup yellow onion, chopped
1 tsp salt
Black pepper
1 tbsp olive oil
1 tsp red pepper flakes
1 tbsp sugar

DIRECTIONS

1. Place a large pot or deep skillet onto the large burner of the stove.

2. Turn the burner on to medium heat. Let the pot or skillet warm for a couple minutes, then add the olive oil.

3. Add in chopped yellow onions. Sauté until the onions are tender.

4. Pour in a can of crushed tomatoes. Stir.

5. Add in basil leaves, red pepper flakes, garlic paste, salt and sugar. Stir well.

6. Taste and add more salt, sugar, or black pepper as needed.

7. Let simmer on medium-low heat for about 10 minutes, stir occasionally.

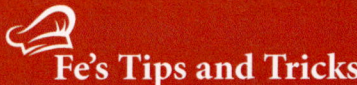

Fe's Tips and Tricks

You can use this red sauce for my "Pizza Pizza" (page 67) and "Pasta Pomodoro" (page 23) recipes.

Pizza! Pizza!

INGREDIENTS

Italian Red Sauce (see recipe on page 65)
Ready-made pizza dough
Olive oil
Mozzarella cheese, shredded
Pizza toppings of your choice

DIRECTIONS

1. Preheat oven to 400 degrees.

2. After you've rolled the pizza dough to your desired thickness and size, spread it on a pizza pan or large baking sheet.

3. Spread the Italian Red Sauce on top.

4. Sprinkle the top of the pizza with cheese to make it as cheesy as you'd like.

5. Add on your favorite toppings.

6. Bake the pizza for about 15-20 minutes. The oven may vary, so check the pizza periodically.

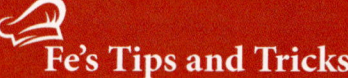

Fe's Tips and Tricks

This recipe calls for pre-made dough, making it a quick and easy meal for even kids to prepare.

Try using various toppings to give your pizza more flair!

Salmon Sushi Bites

Serves 6

INGREDIENTS

Dried seaweed/nori sheets cut into squares
(12 squares)
2 cups brown rice, pre-cooked and cooled
2 skinless salmon filets, cubed small
¼ cup kewpie mayo
1 tbsp sriracha
1 tsp honey
¼ cup green onion, chopped
1 cup avocado, cubed
1 tsp sesame oil
2 tbsp soy sauce
1 tbsp sesame seeds

DIRECTIONS

1. Preheat oven to 350 degrees.

2. Add salmon, soy sauce, green onion, and sesame oil in a large bowl. Gently toss.

3. Using a muffin pan, fill each muffin section with a square nori sheet, topping each with 1 tbsp of rice and a scoop of the salmon mixture.

4. Once the muffin pan is filled, bake in the oven for 15-17 minutes or until the salmon is done.

5. Remove the pan from the oven and set aside.

6. Add the kewpie mayo, sriracha, and honey in a small bowl. Mix. Drizzle this sauce on top of sushi muffins.

Fe's Tips and Tricks

If you're watching your sodium intake, try using low-sodium soy sauce. You'll never know the difference. There's also gluten-free soy sauce.

Authentic sushi rice is made with rice vinegar and sugar. You can substitute brown rice for sushi rice; I prefer brown rice!

Shrimp Sandwich with a Lemon Garlic Aioli

Serves 2

INGREDIENTS

½ pound shrimp, peeled, deveined, and tail off
2 brioche burger buns
1 cup mayo
2 tbsp garlic paste
1 tsp smoked paprika
Arugula
Half a lemon
1 tbsp of butter
Creole seasoning
Black pepper
1 sliced beefsteak tomato

DIRECTIONS

1. In a small bowl, add the mayo, garlic paste, smoked paprika, ½ tsp of black pepper, and a tsp of the juice of half a lemon. Whisk together until the aioli is well-blended and smooth.

2. Lay the shrimp flat on a plate or baking sheet. Sprinkle both sides with Creole seasoning and pepper. Place the shrimp in a heated skillet with a tbsp of butter on medium heat and cook for just a minute or two per side until pink. Remove from heat and set aside.

3. Separate buns. Lightly spray olive oil on the inside of the buns. Place in a heated skillet to the toast inside of the buns.

4. On the bottom side of the bun, smear some aioli sauce onto the top buns. Then top with a bit of arugula, sliced tomato, and the shrimp. Enjoy.

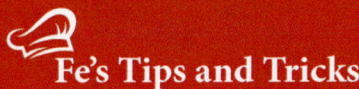 **Fe's Tips and Tricks**

You can replace shrimp with salmon or another meaty white fish (grouper, haddock, cod, etc.)

Add on some avocado for another creamy, fatty element.

The Ultimate Roasted Red Potatoes

INGREDIENTS

3 lb red potatoes, cubed
1 tbsp dried chives
1 tbsp seasoning salt
1 tbsp dried rosemary
1 tbsp smoked paprika
1 tsp black pepper
Olive oil

DIRECTIONS

1. Preheat oven to 425 degrees.

2. Spray or grease the baking sheet with olive oil.

3. Place the potatoes in the oven for 10 minutes.

4. In a small bowl, mix dried chives, seasoning salt, dried rosemary, smoked paprika, and black pepper.

5. Remove the potatoes from the oven and add seasoning mixture to the potatoes.

6. Add the potatoes back to the baking sheet and into the oven. Bake for 10-15 minutes until tender.

Fe's Tips and Tricks

When potatoes sit too long before being cooked, they turn brown. If you're pre-cutting the potatoes and it'll be a while before they cook, add them to a bowl and submerge them in water. This will slow the browning process down.

Do not season your potatoes too soon. The seasonings penetrate the potatoes better once they have cooked a little.

Have you ever added seasonings to vegetables or potatoes early on, and then later, it tasted like nothing was added? Yep, that's why!

Loaded Cheesesteak Potatoes

8 Servings

INGREDIENTS

8 Russet potatoes, washed and dried
2 tsp salt
2 tsp black pepper
2 tsp onion powder
2 tsp garlic powder
1 tsp cayenne pepper
1 lb sliced ribeye or skirt steak
1 cup green bell peppers, sliced
1 cup yellow onion, sliced
½ cup shredded sharp cheddar cheese
½ cup Gruyere cheese, shredded
1 tsp Worcestershire sauce
1 tsp Dijon mustard
⅓ cup dark beer
1 cup milk
¼ cup flour
6 tbsp butter
Canola oil

DIRECTIONS

1. Preheat oven to 400 degrees. Coat each potato with canola oil. Place potatoes directly on the oven rack.

2. Heat a medium saucepan on medium heat. Add the butter. Once melted, add the flour. Whisk the flour until it becomes a paste consistency. Whisk in milk until the flour dissolves, and continue to stir until the milk is thick.

3. In a small bowl, add the garlic powder, onion powder, black pepper, cayenne pepper, and salt. Whisk until the seasonings are well-blended.

4. Add half of the seasoning blend in the saucepan with the milk mixture. Set aside the other half of the seasoning blend.

5. Add sharp cheddar cheese, Gruyere cheese, Worcestershire sauce, and Dijon mustard. Stir until the cheese has melted. Then add in beer and stir again.

6. In a separate bowl, season the steak with the other half of the seasoning blend.

7. Heat a large skillet on medium-high heat. Add 1 tbsp of canola oil and sear steak on both sides for 2-3 minutes until done to your liking. Remove the steak from the skillet and set aside. In the same skillet, sauté peppers and onions until tender.

8. Remove the potatoes from the oven. Potatoes should be crispy externally and soft internally.

9. Split the potatoes. Load potatoes with steak, peppers, onions, and cheese sauce. Then, add additional cheddar and Gruyère cheese on top.

Fe's Tips and Tricks

Well-done steaks have an internal temperature of 165 degrees.
Medium rare is 130-135 degrees.
Medium is 140-145.
Medium-well is 150-155.

Simple Vinaigrette

Serves 8

INGREDIENTS

¼ cup tbsp balsamic vinegar
1 tsp dried oregano
¼ cup extra virgin olive oil
1 tsp salt
½ tsp black pepper

DIRECTIONS

1. In a large bowl, mix together olive oil, balsamic vinegar, dried oregano, salt and black pepper.

2. Tightly cover with Saran Wrap until ready to serve.

Fe's Tips and Tricks

This vinaigrette can be used for just about any salad and some pasta dishes! Check out my Caprese (page 79) and Panzanella Salad (page 81) that use this recipe for the dressing!

Add the juice of half an orange or satsuma for a surprising citrus element and a natural sweetness!

Simple Caprese Salad

Serves 6-8

INGREDIENTS

10 whole basil leaves
8-12 oz mozzarella balls, drained
10 oz grape or cherry tomatoes
½ cup vinaigrette (see page 77)
Salt
Black pepper
Balsamic glaze

DIRECTIONS

1. Halve the cherry or grape tomatoes.

2. In a large bowl, add tomatoes, mozzarella balls, and shredded basil. Mix together.

3. Add the vinaigrette. Salt and pepper to taste. Gently stir.

4. Drizzle with balsamic glaze.

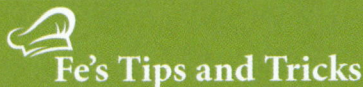

Fe's Tips and Tricks

If you're having difficulty finding the mozzarella balls, purchase the ovalini mozzarella and slice it or pull it apart to make dollops.

Be sure to taste your Caprese Salad before you add salt. The vinaigrette and mozzarella have a fair amount of sodium. You may find that you don't even need it!

Panzanella Salad

INGREDIENTS

1 loaf of French bread, cubed
Olive oil
1 pint grape or cherry tomato medley, halved
Kosher salt
Black pepper
¼ cup red onion, sliced
½ cup English cucumber, sliced
½ tsp Dijon mustard
3 tbsp white wine vinegar
1 tbsp capers
6 fresh basil leaves, shredded
1 tbsp garlic paste
¼ yellow bell pepper, diced
1 tsp honey

DIRECTIONS

Croutons
Preheat the oven to 350 degrees. Line a baking sheet with parchment paper. Arrange French bread cubes on the baking sheet in a single layer and spray or drizzle them with olive oil. Bake for 20-25 minutes or until croutons are toasted.

Salad
In a large bowl, add half of the tomato medley, sliced red onion, English cucumber slices, capers, basil leaves, and diced yellow pepper. Sprinkle with a dash of black pepper. Toss lightly.

Dressing
In a medium bowl, add the garlic paste, Dijon mustard, white wine vinegar, honey, ½ tsp salt, and ½ tsp black pepper. Whisk together. Add dressing to the tomato mixture.

Add the toasted croutons to the tomato mixture, toss, and serve.

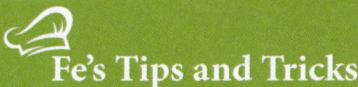

Fe's Tips and Tricks

One of the most incredible things about a Panzanella Salad is that you see a lot of colors and get to taste the different textures.

Be careful with salt when using this recipe. Capers are very salty, so taste before adding salt!

Honey Mustard Dressing

Serves 4

INGREDIENTS

½ cup Dijon mustard
2 tbsp apple cider vinegar
2 tbsp fresh lemon juice
½ cup extra virgin olive oil
1 tsp salt
½ tsp black pepper
4 tbsp honey

DIRECTIONS

1. In a large bowl, mix all ingredients.

2. Tightly cover with Saran wrap until ready to serve.

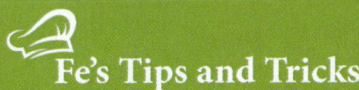

Fe's Tips and Tricks

This honey mustard recipe isn't just for dressing—you could also use it as a light dipping sauce!

Summer Daze Fruit Salad

2-4 Servings

INGREDIENTS

1 cup sliced strawberries
1 cup red grapes
2 cups watermelon chunks
1 cup pineapple chunks
1 cup peeled mandarin wedges
¼ cup honey
1 tsp cinnamon
4 sprigs mint, chopped

DIRECTIONS

1. In a large mixing bowl, add all ingredients and toss together.

2. Serve as is, or add a scoop of sorbet or gelato on top for extra cool points!

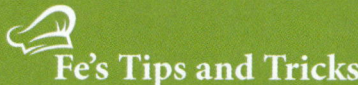

Fe's Tips and Tricks

This fruit salad is like a blank canvas. You can add so many different fruits to it. The main objective is to obtain the different-colored fruits. They each have health benefits!

You can add a scoop of this salad to some carbonated water for a cool fruity drink or juice these fruits and freeze them for a popsicle delight!

Lobster Guacamole

6-8 Servings

INGREDIENTS

3 large ripe avocados, cubed
Salt
Black pepper
2 limes
2 plum tomatoes, diced
¼ cup cilantro, chopped
8 oz Langostino lobster, fully cooked and thawed
1 tbsp Old Bay seasoning
Tortilla chips

DIRECTIONS

1. In a large bowl, add cubed avocados and diced tomatoes. Gently mash the avocado mixture.

2. Add in Langostino lobster and the juice of one lime. Mix.

3. Mix Old Bay seasoning and 1 tsp black pepper. Salt to taste.

4. Serve guacamole with tortilla chips.

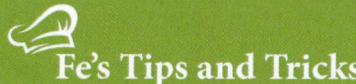

Fe's Tips and Tricks

Langostino lobster can typically be found in the frozen section of stores and seafood markets. If you can't find it, substitute it for another cooked lobster or shrimp!

Try this guacamole with plantain chips as well!

Gelato Dessert

Serves 6-8

INGREDIENTS

1 scoop of gelato
1 can of whipped cream topping
Crushed pineapples and blueberries or
fresh fruit of choice

DIRECTIONS

1. Add a scoop of gelato to a small cup or bowl. Sprinkle with fresh fruit of your choice.

2. Add some whipped cream on top of the gelato and fruit. Add a mint leaf. Enjoy!

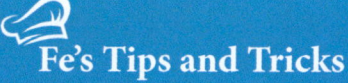

Fe's Tips and Tricks

This dessert will definitely be a household favorite! It's quick, easy, and super delicious!

I teach students to make this dessert at my cooking camps.

Apple Cinnamon Roll Bake

Serves 4

INGREDIENTS

Canned cinnamon rolls
Canned apple filling
Canola oil spray

DIRECTIONS

1. Preheat oven to 350 degrees.

2. Unwrap the cinnamon rolls. Remove the icing that's included. Set the icing aside (you will need it later).

3. Cut the cinnamon rolls into quarters. Place the quarters in a large bowl. Scoop the apple filling from the can into the bowl and gently stir together.

4. Spray the pan. Pour the cinnamon roll mixture into the pan, making sure it's evenly spread.

5. Bake for 40-50 minutes. Make sure that the center of the cinnamon roll is baked through.

6. Remove the pan from the oven. Drizzle icing on top. (Icing comes with the canned cinnamon rolls.)

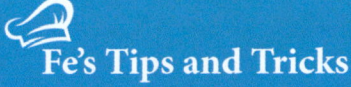

Fe's Tips and Tricks

This recipe is so quick and easy! If you don't want to use apples, you could also use other fruit fillings!

Easy Key Lime Pie

Serves 6

INGREDIENTS

2 cups crushed graham crackers crumbs
6 tbsp salted butter
⅓ cup granulated sugar
¾ cup key lime juice
2 limes
½ cup sour cream
2-14 oz cans of sweetened condensed milk
Canned whipped topping

Fe's Tips and Tricks

Be sure to use actual key lime juice instead of lime juice. Key lime juice has a distinct and more intense acidic flavor.

For a more nutty flavor, try adding grounded walnuts to your crust.

DIRECTIONS

1. Preheat oven to 375 degrees.

2. In a medium bowl, add crushed graham cracker crumbs. Then, add sugar and melted butter. Mix together. Pour the graham cracker mixture into a greased pie dish. Gently press the mixture onto the bottom and sides of the pie dish until it resembles pie crust.

3. Bake pie crust for 8 minutes. Then, set aside to cool.

4. Turn the oven down to 350 degrees once the pie crust is done.

5. Add cans of sweetened condensed milk, sour cream, key lime juice, and zest of two limes in a medium bowl. Mix together.

6. Add the filling to the pie crust. Bake for 10 minutes. Cool in the fridge for 30 minutes.

7. Add some whipped topping on top and serve.

Cinnamon Sugar Apple Pie Tarts

6 Servings

INGREDIENTS

Store-bought puff pastry, thawed
48 thin apple slices (choose your favorite type of apple)
½ cup brown sugar
½ tsp cinnamon
1 tsp lemon juice
1 egg, whisked
Cooking oil spray
Honey

Fe's Tips and Tricks

You can substitute the apples for peaches, pears, and other fruit.

Want to take it a step further and really make this a showstopper?? Make homemade icing with powdered sugar and milk (or water). Drizzle the apple pie tarts with this icing!

DIRECTIONS

1. Preheat oven to 400 degrees.

2. Grease the baking sheet with cooking oil spray.

3. Gently roll out puff pastry. Cut into 6 rectangular pieces of puff pastry.

4. In a bowl, combine apples, cinnamon, sugar, and lemon. Gently toss.

5. Layer apple slices neatly in the middle of each puffy pastry rectangle. It's okay if they overlap a little. (about 6-8 slices per rectangle) Drizzle the remaining cinnamon sugar mixture on top of the apple pastries.

6. Using a basting brush, brush a little of the whisked eggs around the corners and sides of the puff pastry.

7. Bake for 20 minutes or until puff pastry is golden and crispy. Serve with a scoop of ice cream or as is with drizzled honey.

Blueberry Cobbler Overnight Oats

1-2 Servings

INGREDIENTS

2 tbsp fresh blueberries
1 tbsp walnuts, chopped
1 tbsp maple syrup
½ cup rolled oats
½ tsp pure vanilla extract
¼ cup vanilla Greek yogurt
5 ounces vanilla almond milk

DIRECTIONS

1. Combine all the ingredients from the list except the chopped walnuts in a medium bowl. Stir.

2. Add the oatmeal mixture to a jar with a fitted lid. Refrigerate overnight.

3. Remove the lid and top with chopped walnuts. You could also pour the overnight oats into a bowl and stir the walnuts into the overnight oats.

Fe's Tips and Tricks

Blueberries are high in antioxidants and aid in regulating blood sugar. They also help with cholesterol levels, as do oats. You can substitute blueberries with any fruit you'd like. Fruit can also be added right before you consume the overnight oats.

Berry Parfait Trifle

INGREDIENTS

1 pound strawberries, stemless
1 pint fresh blueberries
1 pint fresh blackberries
½ cup raspberry preserves
Water
32 oz vanilla yogurt
8 oz whipped cream topping
Pound cake loaf, Lady Fingers, or granola
Mint (optional)
Honey

ADDITIONAL TOOLS

Trifle bowl or large clear bowl

Fe's Tips and Tricks

Trifles are super easy to make. You can use any fruit you'd like and try different variations! Be careful with bananas unless you will eat them right away; they brown very quickly.

Want to make this even healthier? Ditch the pound cake and use angel food cake! You could also use lady fingers instead of the pound cake.

This also becomes a parfait if you use granola instead of the cake or cookie options.

DIRECTIONS

1. Take your pound cake loaf and cut it into cubes. Set aside.

2. Wash your fruit (strawberries, blueberries and blackberries).

3. Cut your strawberries into halves.

4. In a small microwave-safe bowl, add raspberry preserves and 1 tbsp of water. Gently mix together. Heat in the microwave for about 30 seconds or until the preserves have loosened.

5. In a large bowl, add the strawberries, blueberries, blackberries and raspberry preserves. Gently toss the fresh fruit with the raspberry preserves.

6. In another large bowl, gently fold together yogurt and whipped cream topping.

7. It's time to assemble!

8. In a trifle bowl, add half of your pound cake cubes and half of your fruit mixture on top of the pound cake. Then, add a layer of yogurt mixture (about half). If you have a large enough trifle bowl, do another layer of each. If not, you could build another trifle with the remaining ingredients in a seperate dish.

9. Drizzle with honey and top with a sprig of mint or fruit. Enjoy!

Tropi-Co-Lada Smoothie

Serves 1-2

INGREDIENTS

1 tbsp honey
1 banana
1 cup frozen pineapples
1 cup coconut milk

DIRECTIONS

1. Make sure that your fruit is frozen before preparing the smoothies.

2. Add coconut milk, pineapples, banana, and honey in a blender. Blend until smooth. Garnish with fruit.

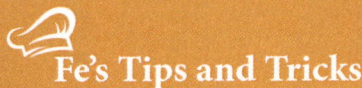

Fe's Tips and Tricks

If you want a thinner consistency, add more coconut milk.

Honey is a powerhouse sweetener! It has several health benefits, including being an antioxidant. Other sweetener options are stevia, agave, and maple syrup.

E's Grown Folk Apple Juice

INGREDIENTS

1.5 oz Crown Royal Apple
½ cup Ginger Ale
Sliced green apple
Mint sprigs

DIRECTIONS

1. In a cocktail glass, add Crown Royal Apple and Ginger Ale. Add in a few ice cubes. Gently stir.

2. Garnish the glass with a green apple slice and a sprig of mint. Enjoy.

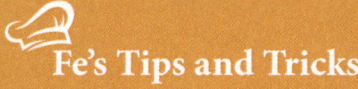

Fe's Tips and Tricks

Pair this drink with my crispy, sticky wings (page 33).

Fe's Raspberry Mule

Serves 1

INGREDIENTS

1 tbsp Raspberry Syrup
Ginger Beer
1.5 oz Vodka (Preferably Ciroc)
Lime slice

DIRECTIONS

1. In a cocktail or mule glass, mix vodka of your choice, raspberry syrup, and ginger beer. Add in a few ice cubes. Gently stir.

   Garnish the glass with a lime slice and a sprig of mint. Enjoy.

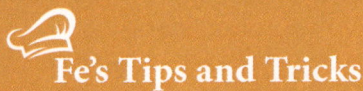

Fe's Tips and Tricks

You can use dehydrated limes as a garnish.

You can dehydrate in your oven if you don't have a dehydrator. Dehydrate fruit under 200 degrees (preferably 150-170). Rotate the fruit every hour for 6-8 hours until the fruit is dry.

This drink pairs well with any seafood or wings dish. Try it with my Honey Sriracha Salmon (page 41).

Tropical White Sangria

6-8 Servings

INGREDIENTS

10 strawberries, chopped
1 cup pineapple, chopped
1 cup mango, chopped
½ cup pineapple juice
¼ cup passion fruit liqueur
6 mint leaves
1 bottle of Pinot Grigio
3 lemon slices

DIRECTIONS

1. Add all ingredients to a large pitcher. Mix.

2. Let the mixture refrigerate for about an hour.

3. Serve in a glass over ice.

Fe's Tips and Tricks

Muddling your fruit will extract more flavor into your sangria. The longer it sits, the more intense it becomes.

Want to skip the ice? Sub frozen fruit for your fruit ingredients. Hold off from adding the frozen fruit until you're ready to serve.

Pair with any Italian dish to complete your meal.

Try it with my Tagliatelle al Ragu (page 37).

What's in Chef Fe's Pantry?

You can tell much about a chef based on what they keep inside their pantry! These are some dry items that Chef Fe keeps on hand!

Seasonings:

Salt
Pepper
Smoked Paprika
Cumin
Creole Seasoning
Bay Leaves
Thyme
Sage
Rosemary
Oregano
Coriander
Fennel Seeds
Garlic Powder
Onion Powder
Turmeric
Cayenne
Gumbo File
Liquid Smoke
Goya All Purpose
Sazon
Bouillon Cubes
Fenugreek Leaves
Curry Powder

Pasta/Grains/Legumes:

Rice (Brown, Basmati, Arborio and Jasmine)
Pasta (Penne, Linguine, Orzo, Pappardelle and Elbow)
Dry Beans (Kidney, Black Eye Peas, Lentils, Lima, and Black Beans)

Thank You!

Of course, I couldn't finish this cookbook without personally thanking you for your support in purchasing this cookbook! Your love and support will not go unnoticed. Please stay tuned to see what more I have in store for all of you FE-Nomenal supporters!

Love, Chef Fe

Stay in Touch

Website: fenomenalcooking.com
Email: thefenomenalcookingexperience@outlook.com
Facebook: The FE-Nomenal Cooking Experience, LLC
Instagram: @thefenomenalcookingexperience

89

15